Citizenship
FOR PRIMARY SCHOOLS

Teacher's Resource Book
Developed by the Institute for Citizenship

Years 1–2

Some material in this Teacher's Book was first published in 1999 by:
The Institute for Citizenship (ISBN 1-9024-8206-9)
Text © Institute for Citizenship 2000
Author: Stephanie Turner
Photographs: © Chris Kelly, except for photographs 1b and10b:
    © Nelson Thornes Ltd 2000

First published in 2000 by:
Stanley Thornes (Publishers) Ltd

Reprinted in 2001 by:
Nelson Thornes Ltd
Delta Place
27 Bath Road
CHELTENHAM
GL53 7TH
United Kingdom

01 02 03 04 05 / 10 9 8 7 6 5 4 3 2

A catalogue record for this book is available from the British Library

ISBN 0-7487-5664-7

Page make-up by Viners Wood Associates.

Printed and bound in Great Britain by Antony Rowe Ltd.

This publication contains material from the Framework for personal, social and health education and citizenship at key stages 1 & 2, produced by the Department for Education and Employment. © Crown copyright. Reproduced under the terms of HMSO Guidance Note 8.

This publication contains material from the Crick Report *Education for Citizenship and the Teaching of Democracy in Schools* (QCA, 1998), reproduced with the permission of the Qualifications and Curriculum Authority.

Resource sheets 1 and 2: information taken from 'Sign Language Link: pocket dictionary of signs', a larger selection of examples can be found on www.deafsign.com, an interactive information and teaching resource on deafness and sign language. Reproduced with permission from Cath Smith, author.
Resource sheet 3: information on the Braille alphabet taken from www.rnib.org.uk, reproduced by permission of the RNIB.

The Institute for Citizenship and Nelson Thornes Ltd wish to thank all those who have helped with the development of the Citizenship Project. Staff and pupils in the five pilot schools:
    Elsa Baird, Whipperley Infant School, Luton
    Julia Bowles, Warden Hill Infant School, Luton
    Deborah Cochrane, Bramingham Primary School, Luton
    Lynn Collett, Icknield Infant School, Luton
    Janice Dines, Wigmore Primary School, Luton and
    Luton Borough Council Education Department.

Staff and pupils in the schools where the photographs were taken:
    Icknield Infant School, Luton
    Norton St Nicholas CE Primary School, Letchworth Garden City
    Whipperley Infant School, Luton

We also acknowledge the support of The Equitable Charitable Trust and Whitbread in the Community for funding the development work for this project in Luton.

Contents   Page

Foreword by
Professor Bernard Crick

(The full weight of the government is now behind preparing all our nation's children to be active and responsible citizens in adult life. Part of that is giving children from the earliest age some of the experiences, skills, knowledge and values needed to achieve that end. A lot of the guidance and resources needed for schools will be delivered by expert voluntary groups, to avoid detailed central direction. This primary school project from the Institute for Citizenship is one of the best I have seen, both in content and design.

Professor Bernard Crick
Chairman of the advisory group which reported as Education for Citizenship and the Teaching of Democracy in Schools, and former adviser to the DfEE on Citizenship.

Introduction

We are all citizens and citizenship education begins at an early age. This 'Citizenship for Primary Schools' project helps teachers to begin citizenship education at Key Stage 1 with Year 1 and 2 children. For the first time, citizenship is included in the revised National Curriculum and will be taught across all Key Stages. Teachers will recognise much that is now labelled as citizenship education as good practice already in primary schools. In planning citizenship education a first step will often be an audit of citizenship education already taking place under whatever label. 'Citizenship for Primary Schools' at Key Stage 1 consists of a Flipover Book of sixteen photographs of children as active citizens and this Teacher's Resource Book. The project aims to stimulate an interest in beginning and developing citizenship education with the youngest children.

Citizenship in the National Curriculum 2000

The National Curriculum Handbook for primary teachers in England includes a *Framework for personal, social and health education and citizenship at key stages 1 and 2*. There are non-statutory guidelines for citizenship. Section 2 is headed 'Preparing to play an active role as citizens'. Section 5 is headed 'Breadth of opportunities'. The National Curriculum charts throughout this Teacher's Resource Book clearly show which parts of sections 2 and 5 are being addressed by each set of activities. A copy of the relevant part of the National Curriculum at Key Stage 1 is included as Appendix 1.

The National Curriculum for Citizenship is based on the Crick Report *Education for Citizenship and the Teaching of Democracy in Schools* published by the Qualifications and Curriculum Authority (QCA) in September 1998. This report includes the 'learning outcomes' that may be expected at the end of each Key Stage. Each of the sections in this Teacher's Resource Book shows which of the Crick Report's learning outcomes will be achieved; as these outcomes are regarded as best practice in citizenship education. A copy of the relevant part of the Crick Report at Key Stage 1 is included as Appendix 2.

The integration of citizenship education into the curriculum is left up to schools. It is already embedded in personal, social and health education (PSHE). The use of assemblies and circle time for effective citizenship education is another possibility. However, from now on, citizenship as a distinct subject will have a regular place on the timetable and will pervade all aspects of school life.

Good Practice in Citizenship Education

An active citizen is someone who plays a part in society. To encourage active citizenship, children need to participate, to learn by doing, to be given responsibility appropriate to their age and to play an active part in their own learning. In short, they need to learn the skills of active citizenship. Professor Crick in his report (September 1998) defines citizenship education as social and moral responsibility, political literacy and community involvement. Only the second strand may be new to primary teachers, though the third may be a challenge to achieve.

Good practice in citizenship education includes many of the following:
- A programme of study which begins with the individual child, their needs and who provides for those needs at home, at school, locally and nationally.
- Opportunities for children to participate in class, defining rules, representing each other, contributing to the life of the school.
- A school council, with a clearly defined remit, and where each class is represented.
- A school environmental policy, developed by the children as part of lessons in science, geography, maths and English, which all pupils work to implement.
- School buildings and grounds that are cared for by the children.
- Links with the local authority: children make regular visits to the council chamber to take part in their own debates as well as to find out about local government.
- Councillors are invited into school to talk with children about their role. Teachers may want to approach school governors who are also councillors.
- Links with the local planning department so that planners may help children with role-playing real issues or practise resolving planning dilemmas.
- Visitors from local and national voluntary bodies are welcomed into school to work with the children so that the children gain an understanding of their work, and of the role of volunteers.
- Parents are welcomed into the school to explain their role in the wider community, for example, as members of community groups or local businesses.
- School governors are asked to explain their role to children.
- Ongoing citizenship education is taught throughout every class every week. Citizenship education is not simply allocated a slot in the timetable, but pervades the ethos of the school.

Guide to Using the Photographs

For each photograph, the guidance begins with the 'Aims' and 'Questions' to stimulate discussion. Next are 'Activities' for using the photographs to encourage citizenship education with children. Then there are 'Extension Activities' as the photographs lead on to other citizenship work. 'Watch Points' provide additional teacher support on any issues that may require further explanation or research. Finally, a table shows which aspects of the National Curriculum and the Crick Report are fulfilled.

Other Activities Using the Photographs

A number of generic activities could be used with any or all of the photographs. The links to other subjects in the National Curriculum are given on page 37, but links to English are particularly strong in most aspects of citizenship education, as shown in these generic activities. Some of these activities may serve as an introduction to citizenship education, while Activity 6 would provide a useful summary of work covered.

1. Describing Photographs
Children are asked to describe what is happening in the photograph to encourage observation, speaking and listening.

2. Telling Stories

Children are asked to tell the story of the photograph from the point of view of one of the participants.

3. What Happens Next?

Children make up a story about what happens next, or they can role-play what happens next.

4. Speech Bubbles

Children may be helped to put words into the mouths of the children in the photographs. This can be done literally with large pieces of paper cut to shape.

5. Questions

Children suggest questions they would like to ask the children in the photographs. In an additional activity children could formulate the answers to these questions.

6. Design a Game

With the children, design a game based on a numbered route and chance squares or chance cards. For example, create a route of twenty numbered squares, from school to a special local place. Then use dice or spinners to follow the route. Mark some squares as special; on these children can turn over an 'Active Citizen Card' to move forward an extra square. Ask the children to suggest the content for the Active Citizen Cards, which can change each time the game is played.

Active Citizenship

As the Teacher's Resource Book will show, active citizenship needs to be encouraged, celebrated and rewarded. Acknowledging active citizenship could be a regular part of the 'good work assembly'. Certificates, stars or stickers could be awarded to members of each class each week, both as a reward and as a reminder to others. (The Institute for Citizenship can supply 'I am an Active Citizen' stickers if required.) Displays of citizenship work will inform parents and visitors to the school of the importance attached to this work.

Schools should try to involve parents in citizenship education. Parents can help and support citizenship education in schools and be a link to the local community. Schools may also benefit from the support of the local authority, local and national voluntary bodies and other interested persons. Teachers should maximise the use of all resources available, including human resources.

This citizenship project is based on photographs of children as active citizens. All aspects of active citizenship can start from the photographs and the 'Extension Activities' lead to the development of a full citizenship curriculum.

Stories can provide another effective way to introduce citizenship education, and many stories for young children carry a strong message. A table of links to other National Curriculum subjects is included on page 37. This Teacher's Resource Book then gives background information for teachers on some of the topics covered. There is a Sources of Information table (page 42) and a list of useful organisations (page 43).

1 Helping

Aims
- To consider who helps children and how they help each other
- To introduce the concept of citizenship
- To foster a sense of responsibility for self and for others
- To link to services provided by the local community

Questions
1. What is happening in this photograph?
2. Who is helping whom?
3. Who helps the children in the classroom, at school, at home, elsewhere?
4. Who do the children themselves help at school, at home, elsewhere?

Activities
- Make a list of any chores or jobs that members of the class do around the home and garden. Do they 'work' for pocket money or help to be kind? Does pocket money have to be earned?
- Consider what help is provided to pupils and their families impersonally, such as libraries, sports facilities or rubbish removal.
- Consider who provides this help and how it is organised by the local council.
- Identify any links to the local authority, such as family members employed, services used and places visited.
- Make a list of recent visitors to your school. Why did they visit and how did the children help them? Who else could be invited?

Extension Activities
- Invite a school governor who is also a councillor to visit the class to tell the children about their work and to answer the children's questions.
- Arrange a visit to the council chamber, library or other significant building.
- Follow the Town Trail if there is one, or make one up in your area.

Watch Points
- See background information on pages 37–38.

1a:
The classroom assistant is helping two boys with their reading. The two girls are helping each other.

1b:
Children welcoming a visitor to their school.

National Curriculum

Preparing to play an active role as citizens

Pupils should be taught:

2f that they belong to various groups and communities, such as family and school
2i to realise that money comes from different sources and can be used for different purposes.

Breadth of Opportunities

Pupils should be taught through opportunities to:

5e meet and talk with people
5g consider social and moral dilemmas that they come across in everyday life (for example, use of money)
5h ask for help.

Best Practice (Crick Report)

Skills and Aptitudes

- Reflect on issues of social and moral concern.

Knowledge and Understanding

- Know where they live, in relation to their local and national community, understand that there are different types and groups of people living in their local community.

- Know about the different kinds of relationships which exist between adults and pupils.

2 Using Sign Language

Aims

- To encourage consideration for others
- To encourage inclusion of everyone in the class
- To consider the needs of others

Questions

1. Why does the boy use sign language?
2. Why is the girl using sign language?
3. Why is it important that all pupils in this class learn sign language?
4. Are there any pupils in your class who need special help?
5. How do you help other members of your class?

Activities

- Invite someone to the school to demonstrate sign language.
- Invite someone who has a guide dog to visit the class to explain what it is like to be blind.
- Role-play helping other people. Find out if help is needed and how best to help.
- Drama: act out befriending a new member of the class.
- Tell a story about helping.

Extension Activities

- Teach the class sign language using Resource Sheets 1 and 2.
- Make cards of Braille letters or numbers using Resource Sheet 3 and look out for Braille on lifts or products such as bleach.
- Ask the children to cover their eyes or ears with their hands. How does it feel to be without one of their senses?
- Give instructions in a different language. How does it feel not to understand?

Watch Points

- You might want to go through these basic guidelines for communicating with deaf people:
  - Make good eye contact.
  - Face the person, so that they may read your lips.
  - Learn British Sign Language.
- See background information on page 38.

2:
The boy is deaf. The girl is communicating with him using sign language.

National Curriculum

Preparing to play an active role as citizens

Pupils should be taught:

2e to realise that people and other living things have needs, and that they have responsibilities to meet them.

Breadth of Opportunities

Pupils should be taught through opportunities to:

5a take and share responsibility.

Best Practice (Crick Report)

Skills and Aptitudes

- Use imagination when considering the experience of others.

- Reflect on issues of social and moral concern.

Knowledge and Understanding

- Understand the different kinds of responsibility that they take on, in helping others or respecting differences.

- Understand the meaning of respect/disrespect, similar/different.

3 Excluding and Including

Aims
- To encourage consideration for others
- To include and involve everyone
- To consider the needs of others

Questions
1. What is the group of children doing?
2. What has happened to the girl?
3. How do you think the girl feels?
4. Has something like this ever happened to you or your friend?
5. How can you make sure that no one is left out in your class?
6. What could the girl do to help matters?
7. Refer to photograph 3b. How is this photograph different and what is good about it?

Activities
- Role-play the scene in photograph 3a and what you think happens next.
- Tell a story about asking someone to join in.
- Write a play, based on the scene in photograph 3a, with a happy ending.
- Discuss bullying and what can be done to prevent it.
- Discuss consideration for the needs and feelings of others.
- How can a group of friends make sure that no one is left out or bullied?

Extension Activities
- Discuss what leads people to join groups, both formal and informal.
- Make a list of groups that class members belong to.

Watch Points
- Use the opportunity to remind children of school policies on behaviour and bullying.
- Respect for each other will suggest the best way to behave.

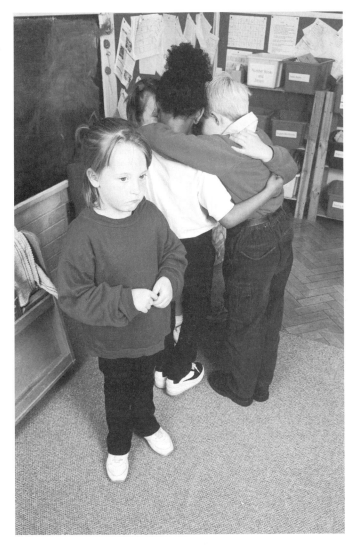

3b:
Children playing together on a climbing frame.

3a:
Four friends are huddled together sharing a secret or having fun. One girl is excluded from the group.

National Curriculum

Preparing to play an active role as citizens

Pupils should be taught:

2e to realise that people and other living things have needs, and that they have responsibilities to meet them.

Breadth of Opportunities

Pupils should be taught through opportunities to:

5a take and share responsibility.

Best Practice (Crick Report)

Skills and Aptitudes

• Use imagination when considering the experience of others.

• Reflect on issues of social and moral concern and 'real life' incidents.

Knowledge and Understanding

• Recognise how the concept of fairness can be applied.

• Understand the different kinds of responsibility that they take on in helping others.

• Understand language: happy/sad, upset, shy.

4 Sharing Special Occasions

Aims
- To understand and share a different culture
- To understand the role of special food and special clothes

Questions
1. What is the girl who is standing doing?
2. What are the other children doing?
3. What do you notice about the food?
4. What do you notice about the clothing?

Activities
- Talk about special food within families and how it differs from other food.
- Discuss and contrast the special food of different cultures.
- Discuss respect for, and being open to, different customs and good manners when tasting unfamiliar foods.
- Arrange for children to bring food to share.
- Contrast different types of special clothing, for example, wedding dress, party clothes, clothes for religious occasions.

Extension Activities
- Invite parents to come in to school to cook special food with children.
- Design a special menu and invitations.
- Arrange a tea party and invite the school's neighbours as well as parents.
- Arrange a fashion show of special clothes.

Watch Points
- The photograph shows one of many different cultures in the UK. For some children the food and dress will be familiar; for others it will be new and different. The photograph serves as a stimulus from which the children find out about cultures that are different from their own.
- The dress the girl is wearing is called a 'Shalwar Kameez'.
- The food the children are sharing is pakora and pilau rice. Other Muslim food includes barfi, a traditional sweet made with milk, sugar and flavourings such as coconut.
- The Halal is a guide for Muslims as to what they should and should not eat.
- See background information on pages 38–39.

4:
The mother of the Pakistani Muslim girl, who is standing, has made food for the class to share. The girl is wearing her best dress, which she wears for the Festival of Eid ul-Fitr. She is telling her classmates about the dress and the food.

National Curriculum

Preparing to play an active role as citizens

Pupils should be taught:

2f that they belong to various groups and communities, such as family and school.

Breadth of Opportunities

Pupils should be taught through opportunities to:

5f develop relationships through work and play.

Best Practice (Crick Report)

Skills and Aptitudes

• Work with others and gather their opinions.

Knowledge and Understanding

• Know about differences and similarities between people and understand that many of these differences are linked with cultural and religious diversity.

5 Explaining Culture

<table>
<tr><td>

Aims

</td><td>

- To understand and share a different culture
- To respect the religious customs of others

</td></tr>
<tr><td>

Questions

</td><td>

1. What is the boy who is kneeling doing?
2. What is the boy who is standing doing?
3. Why are only boys involved?
4. What is the importance of the carpet?
5. Why is it important to understand and respect different racial and cultural groups?

</td></tr>
<tr><td>

Activities

</td><td>

- Ask members of the class to talk about the religious and cultural practices they are familiar with.
- Make and illustrate a calendar with the important dates for all the cultures in your class. (See the 'Contact List' on page 44 for the address of The Shap Working Party on World Religions in Education.)
- List the similarities between cultures as well as the differences.

</td></tr>
<tr><td>

Extension Activities

</td><td>

- Discuss which buildings and special places are important to different faiths, for example, mosque, church, temple, Mecca, Jerusalem, Bethlehem.
- Visit local places of worship.

</td></tr>
<tr><td>

Watch Points

</td><td>

- The photograph shows one of many different cultures in the UK. For some children the act of worship will be familiar; for others it will be new and different. The photograph serves as a stimulus from which the children find out about cultures that are different from their own.
- The Muslim faith considers it inappropriate for women to pray with men. Women are able to pray separately with other women.
- When arranging to visit local places of worship, ask the children for their suggestions. Which places of worship do they attend?
- See background information on pages 38–39.

</td></tr>
</table>

5:
One Turkish Muslim boy is demonstrating his prayers on a prayer mat. Another boy is explaining to his classmates. They are wearing prayer caps and have removed their shoes. The prayer mat incorporates a compass so it can be oriented to Mecca.

National Curriculum

Preparing to play an active role as citizens

Pupils should be taught:

2f that they belong to various groups and communities, such as family and school.

Breadth of Opportunities

Pupils should be taught through opportunities to:

5f develop relationships through work and play.

Best Practice (Crick Report)

Skills and Aptitudes

- Use imagination when considering the experience of others.

Knowledge and Understanding

- Know about differences and similarities between people and understand that many of these differences are linked with cultural and religious diversity.

6 Caring for the Environment

Aims
- To study the environment
- To care for our surroundings
- To value the natural environment

Questions
1. Where are these children and what are they doing?
2. What might they see in the pond?
3. How do you help care for the environment?
4. What can you see that attracts wildlife?
5. How can you help to care for your school environment?

Activities
- Visit your school's nature garden to see what animal and plant life is there.
- Draw the view from the classroom window and then another picture of how you would like it to be.
- Go on an environmental walk to observe surroundings at different seasons.
- Discuss how you can help care for the environment, including recycling, reusing, conserving and using resources in a sustainable way.
- Discuss vandalism and how to encourage responsible behaviour.
- Develop a school environmental policy through work in maths, English, science and geography. (See Resource Sheet 4.)

Extension Activities
- Plan and develop a nature garden if you do not have one already.
- Set up recycling facilities and a compost heap at school.
- Make use of opportunities in your area such as a visit to a recycling centre, or a visit from a science recycling van or from a theatre group with an environmental theme.
- Conduct a playground survey and plan improvements.
- Discuss the need for conservation of the natural environment, the economic costs of this and who should pay for it.

Watch Points
- In carrying out nature garden activities, it is, of course, necessary to make a simple risk assessment, to consider health and safety and adequate adult supervision.
- See background information on page 39.

6:
The children help to care for the school's nature garden, so that it is a haven for wildlife. Here they are looking for signs of life in the pond.

National Curriculum

Preparing to play an active role as citizens

Pupils should be taught:

2g what improves or harms their local, natural and built environments and about some of the ways people look after them
2i to realise that money comes from different sources and can be used for different purposes.

Breadth of Opportunities

Pupils should be taught through opportunities to:

5a take and share responsibility
5d make real choices (for example, how to spend and save money sensibly)
5g consider social and moral dilemmas that they come across in everyday life (for example, simple environmental issues).

Best Practice (Crick Report)

Skills and Aptitudes

• Reflect on issues of social and moral concern.

Knowledge and Understanding

• Understand the different kinds of responsibility that they take on in looking after shared property.

7 Discussing and Working in Pairs

Aims

- To encourage children to express themselves and speak clearly
- To encourage children to listen to each other
- To encourage respect for the views of others

Questions

1. What are the children doing?
2. Why are they talking to each other?
3. Why is it important to learn to listen?
4. What can you say if you disagree with what is being said?
5. How can you show that you are listening to someone?
6. How is it helpful to work together?
7. Is it easier or more difficult to work together?

Activities

- Ask children to discuss an issue in pairs.
- Ask one pair to join another pair to widen the discussion.
- Ask one child to relay the views of their partner to the rest of the class.
- Arrive at a consensus of views within the class.
- Talk about the vocabulary necessary to express agreement and dissent.

Extension Activities

- Start with a practical activity to give the children something to talk about. It could be tidying the home corner or finding information. Do a task individually, then in pairs and then discuss the advantages and disadvantages of different ways of working.

Watch Points

- Encourage children to disagree with ideas rather than a person, and to remain friends even if they think differently.
- Learn to say "I think that ..." and recognise that there are other opinions.
- Learn to say "I don't agree ..." rather than "You are wrong".
- The children may suggest different ways of showing you are listening to someone: by smiling, by making eye contact, by gestures such as nodding.

7a:
The children are discussing the books they have been reading. They are learning to talk and to listen.

7b:
Two children are working together, helping each other with maths bricks.

National Curriculum

Preparing to play an active role as citizens

Pupils should be taught:

2a to take part in discussions with one other person and the whole class.

Breadth of Opportunities

Pupils should be taught through opportunities to:

5b feel positive about themselves
5c take part in discussions.

Best Practice (Crick Report)

Skills and Aptitudes

- Express and justify a personal opinion.

- Contribute to a paired discussion, learning to take turns and respond to the views of others.

Knowledge and Understanding

- Know and understand through the process of exploratory talk, the meaning of respect/ disrespect, question, comment, discuss, agree/ disagree, opinion.

8 Debating

Aims
- To understand that different types of discussions require different structures
- To understand the need for and advantages of formal debate
- To compare class debates with debates in council and parliament

Questions
1. What is happening in this photograph?
2. Why are the children sitting in two lines?
3. Why is one boy sitting on a chair and what does he do?
4. Why is one boy holding a piece of paper?

Activities
- Hold an unstructured whole class discussion to demonstrate that it is difficult for everyone to express his or her point of view.
- Show the value of having a chairperson, formal structure and time limits.
- Hold a simple debate about a topic such as school dinners versus packed lunches or a separate infant school versus a combined primary school.
- Ask the children if they know of any topical issues in the town?
- Make the connection with debates in the local council chamber and in parliament.

Extension Activities
- Debate other topics to give all children the opportunity to play different roles: supermarket versus corner shop, playing outside versus watching TV, building new houses versus setting land aside for play.
- Visit the local council chamber and conduct your debate there.
- See background information on pages 37–38 and 40–41.

8:
The children are sitting formally in lines to symbolise two sides of a debate. One pupil is the chairperson.

National Curriculum

Preparing to play an active role as citizens

Pupils should be taught:

2b to take part in a simple debate about topical issues.

Breadth of Opportunities

Pupils should be taught through opportunities to:

5c take part in discussions
5g consider social and moral dilemmas that they come across in everyday life.

Best Practice (Crick Report)

Skills and Aptitudes

• Take part in a simple debate and vote on an issue.

9 School Council Meeting

Aims
- To understand the purpose of a formal meeting
- To understand how to conduct a meeting
- To learn to represent the views of others
- To contribute to the life of the class and school

Questions
1. What do you think is happening here?
2. What is the woman doing?
3. What is the girl with the notebook and pencil doing?
4. Why do we need a record of a meeting?

Activities
- Set up a class council with elected representatives. (See the 'Contact List' on page 44 for the address of Schools Council UK.)
- Discuss the qualities needed and the responsibility of representing others.
- Give the class council some responsibility, for example, for doing daily jobs such as setting up the computer, getting out books, pencils and other materials at different times, and organising others in putting things away.
- Have several meetings so that everyone gets a turn.
- Discuss topics suggested by the class and agree implementation.

Extension Activities
- Set up a school council with elected representatives from each class.
- Give the council a clear remit so that it is more than a discussion forum.
- Give the school council a project to work on for a term.
- Give the school council a small amount of money to spend on improvements in school, so that children arrive at a consensus of how to spend it wisely.
- See background information on page 40.

9:
The children are having a meeting with a classroom helper, who is the chairperson. One girl is taking minutes and another child is speaking.

National Curriculum

Preparing to play an active role as citizens

Pupils should be taught:

2h to contribute to the life of the class and school
2i to realise that money comes from different sources and can be used for different purposes

Breadth of Opportunities

Pupils should be taught through opportunities to:

5d make real choices (for example, how to spend and save money sensibly)
5g consider social and moral dilemmas that they come across in everyday life

Best Practice (Crick Report)

Skills and Aptitudes

- Work with others and gather their opinions in an attempt to meet a challenge of shared significance.

Knowledge and Understanding

- Know about the different kinds of relationships which exist between adults and pupils, and that the power in such relationships can be exercised responsibly.

10 Making School and Safety Rules

Aims
- To understand the need for codes of behaviour or rules
- To contribute to forming class and school rules
- To compare rules in school with laws in society
- To understand the value of other rules such as safety rules

Questions
1. What are the rules in your class and school?
2. Why do we need to have rules in school and elsewhere?
3. Which rules are easy to keep and which more difficult?
4. How do you help to decide what the rules should be?
5. Refer to photo 10b. Why is it important to find a safe place and to cross the road only when told to do so?
6. Refer to photo 10b. What safety features can you see in the photograph?

Activities
- Start from scratch without rules and invent new ones.
- Role-play situations without rules or a game without a referee.
- Brainstorm a list of rules. Later, ask "What are the rules?". Which have been remembered? Show the importance of a few easily remembered rules.

Extension Activities
- Make the connection with laws made in parliament.
- Discuss how society enforces its laws and why.
- Make the link to the Ten Commandments and the laws or codes of other faiths.

Watch Points
- You could discuss the laws or codes of other faiths, including the 'Five Pillars' of Islam, the 'Torah' of Judaism, the 'Guru Granth Sahib' (holy book) of Sikhism, the 'Dharma' of Hinduism.
- The Green Cross Code – Stop! Look! Listen! – is the key to road safety.
- Safety features include the school crossing patrol, 'Stop' sign, special road surface and reflective clothing.
- Note the link between photograph 10b, photograph 1a 'Helping' and photograph 1b 'Welcoming a Visitor'.
- See background information on page 40.

10b:
These children are learning to cross the road safely with the help of the school crossing patrol.

10a:
At this school, the five golden rules are displayed on every classroom wall: talk quietly, be helpful, walk in school, think about others, always do your best.

National Curriculum

Preparing to play an active role as citizens

Pupils should be taught:

2c to recognise choices they can make, and recognise the difference between right and wrong
2d to agree and follow rules for their group and classroom, and understand how rules help them.

Breadth of Opportunities

Pupils should be taught through opportunities to:

5a take and share responsibility (for example, for their own behaviour; by helping to make classroom rules and following them).

Best Practice (Crick Report)

Knowledge and Understanding

- Know about rules in the classroom, how to frame rules, that different rules serve different purposes.

- Understand different kinds of behaviour using moral categories.

11 Voting

Aims
- To have the opportunity to vote
- To understand the purpose of a secret ballot

Questions
1. What are the children in the queue doing?
2. What is the boy sitting at the front doing?
3. What do voting, election, ballot box and ballot paper mean?
4. Why do we have a secret ballot?

Activities
- Hold a class election to elect a boy and a girl as class leaders for a week or longer. The vote could be by show of hands or by secret ballot. What can the leaders do for the class community? They represent those who did not vote for them as well as those who did.
- Give the class leaders clear responsibilities, for example, collecting the register, leading the class into assembly, watering the plants.
- Explain majority decisions and democracy.
- Use voting to help the class make choices, for example, about what to do at certain times.

Extension Activities
- Elect a Head Girl and a Head Boy with responsibilities in the school.
- Make the connections between the election and the local council.
- Invite the Mayor or Council chairperson to visit your school.
- Make the connections with recent elections:
    May 2000: Election of Mayor for London and London Assembly
    May 2000: Local elections in some local authorities in England
    May 1999: Local elections, Scottish Parliament, Welsh Assembly
    June 1999: European Parliament
- Explore relevant vocabulary: MP Member of Parliament, MEP Member of the European Parliament, House of Commons, House of Lords, Act of Parliament, Law.

Watch Points
- A ballot vote is usually a secret vote – it is a vote on a piece of paper that is put into a box.
- A secret vote by ballot helps ensure anonymous voting and reduces the risk of voters being bribed or threatened.
- See background information on pages 37–38 and 40–41.

11:
The children are queuing up to place their ballot papers in the ballot box. The girl is an election official. The boy sitting at the front is placing a cross on his ballot paper.

National Curriculum

Preparing to play an active role as citizens

Pupils should be taught:

2h to contribute to the life of the class and school.

Breadth of Opportunities

Pupils should be taught through opportunities to:

5d make real choices.

Best Practice (Crick Report)

Skills and Aptitudes

• Take part in a simple debate and vote on an issue.

12 Being a European Citizen

Aims
- To set work on the local area in a wider context
- To introduce the idea of European citizenship

Questions
1. What are the children doing and where does the map show?
2. Do any of the children in the class or their parents come from another European country?
3. Have any children in the class visited another European country on holiday?

Activities
- Locate all the places in Europe with which members of the class have some connection.
- Measure the distances from your town to some of these places using a piece of string, and compare with distances to, say, Edinburgh or Cardiff.
- On an outline map of Europe colour and name the countries which are part of the European Union. (See background information on page 41.)

Extension Activities
- Read folk stories from other countries.
- Collect artefacts from different countries and assemble them round the map and link them to the relevant countries.
- Link to the wider world and the United Nations. The easiest way to do this is to invite an education officer from one of the voluntary organisations to work with your class. (This will not be fund raising or propaganda but education in its widest sense. See the list of useful organisations on pages 43–44.)
- See background information on page 41.

12:
The children are studying a map of Europe.

National Curriculum

Preparing to play an active role as citizens

Pupils should be taught:

2f that they belong to various groups and communities, such as family and school

Breadth of Opportunities

Pupils should be taught through opportunities to:

5c take part in discussions (for example, talking about topics of school, local, national, European and global concern).

Best Practice (Crick Report)

Skills and Aptitudes

- Use imagination when considering the experience of others.

Knowledge and Understanding

- Know where they live, in relation to their local and national community.

1 Sign Language

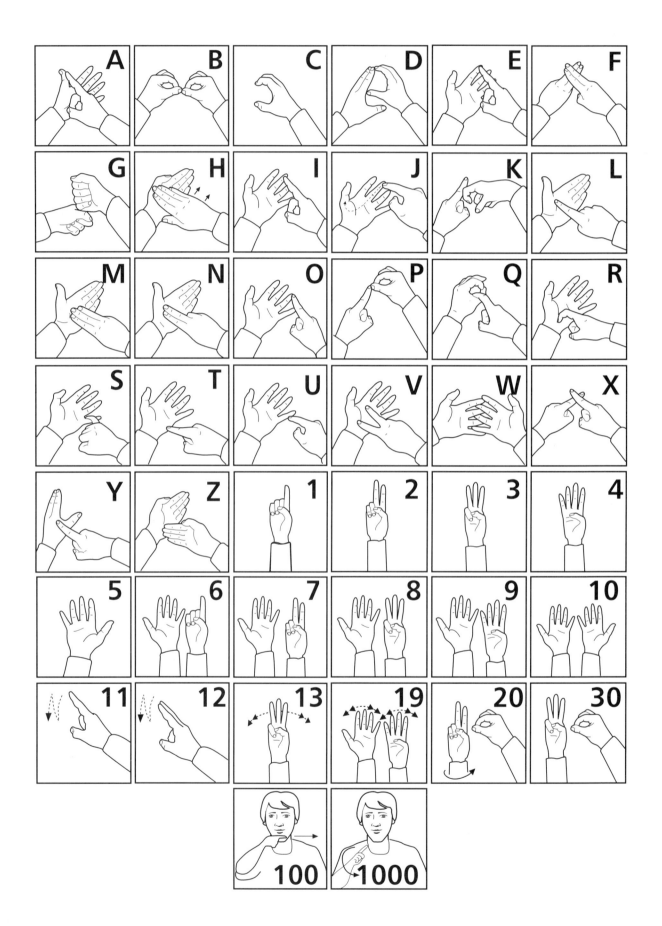

2 Sign Language

Good, great or hello

Closed hand with thumb extended and up, makes small firm forward movement. *NOTES*: this sign is also a common greeting sign in the Deaf community. *VARIATIONS*: open hand palm forward, pointing up, twists at the wrist, closing to thumb up palm left. Both hands can be used for extra emphasis.

Name or to be called

Tips of extended fingers of 'N' hand contact side of forehead, then the hand moves and twists forward/down. *VARIATION*: Closed hands with index and middle fingers extended and open are held with palms facing each other, then move apart slightly as the fingers flex. This version also means CALLED, TITLE, TOPIC. *NOTES*: It is common in Deaf culture to give people 'name signs' based on some feature or characteristic.

I or me

Tip of extended index finger contacts the front of the chest.

Please or if you please

Fingertips of flat hand contact the chin, then hand moves forward/down as fingers close onto the palm. Can be made without the final closing movement, also meaning THANKS, THANK YOU.

3 Braille

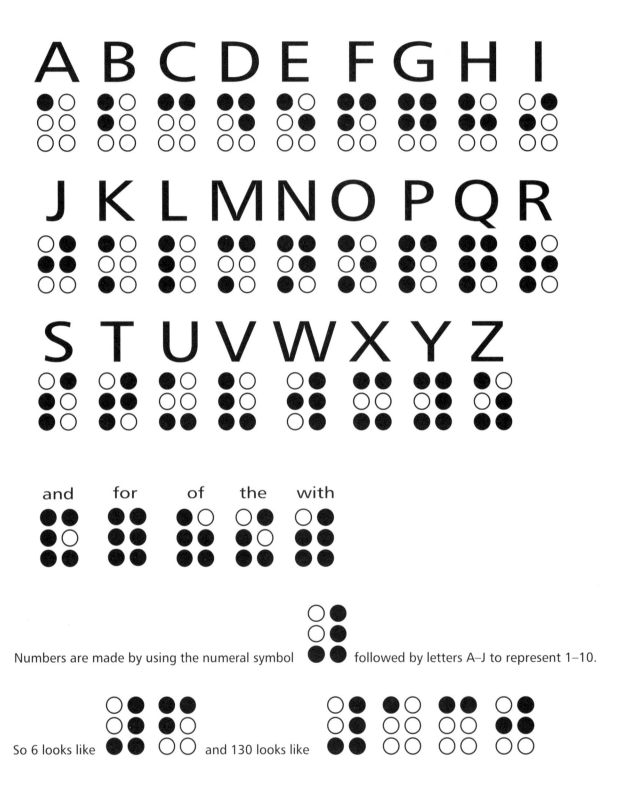

Numbers are made by using the numeral symbol ⠼ followed by letters A–J to represent 1–10.

So 6 looks like ⠼⠋ and 130 looks like ⠼⠁⠉⠚

4 Caring for the Environment

The natural environment

One of the best ways of encouraging interest in and care for the environment is for children to be given some responsibility for cultivating plants. It may be a few plants or a tray of seeds on the classroom windowsill, or their own garden within the school grounds. The children can then learn to feed, water and protect the plants.

From their own gardening they can begin to appreciate the need to care for the school grounds and public natural areas. Essentially, this care will be not damaging plants including trees, not leaving litter and not walking on the soil, but keeping to the paths.

It is not recommended that schools keep pets, but rather that they provide suitable habitats to encourage wildlife. A corner left wild for nettles to thrive will encourage insects, butterflies and birds. Wild bird food, not bread, can be provided in the winter to further encourage wildlife. The conservation charities in the Contact List (pages 43–44) can assist schools in the development and management of their grounds.

The built environment

Children can begin to appreciate the built environment by taking care of their classroom and school. They should be encouraged to put litter in the bin and food waste in the compost bin. They can learn to keep things tidy and clean.

Recycling

The school can give a lead by purchasing recycled products, especially paper. Children can be encouraged to recycle, to reuse or even to refuse unnecessary consumption. It is recommended that schools join any local recycling schemes, and, if necessary, provide containers on site for collecting waste paper, cans and glass. The way the school itself behaves will reflect the curriculum being taught. It may be possible to make a small amount of money from recycling, though this is not the primary reason for doing it. If so, then the children, through the school council, could share in decisions to spend the money earned on environment improvements. Your local council may be willing to supply special recycling bins, or will be able to tell you of local voluntary schemes.

Key Stage 1 Citizenship Curriculum Matrix

Developing confidence and responsibility and making the most of their abilities

Photo	1	1b	2	3	3b	4	5	6	7	7b	8	9	10	10b	11	12
1a					•								•	•		
1b									•	•	•					
1c																
1d																
1e																

Preparing to play an active role as citizens

Photo	1	1b	2	3	3b	4	5	6	7	7b	8	9	10	10b	11	12
2a									•	•						
2b											•					
2c					•								•	•		
2d													•	•		
2e			•	•	•											
2f	•	•				•	•									•
2g								•								
2h												•			•	
2i	•							•				•				

Developing good relationships and respecting the differences between people

Photo	1	1b	2	3	3b	4	5	6	7	7b	8	9	10	10b	11	12
4a		•		•												
4b									•	•						
4c						•	•									
4d	•	•														
4e				•	•											

Breadth of opportunities

Photo	1	1b	2	3	3b	4	5	6	7	7b	8	9	10	10b	11	12
5a			•	•	•			•					•	•		
5b									•	•						
5c									•	•						•
5d								•				•			•	
5e	•	•					•									
5f						•	•			•						
5g	•	•			•			•				•	•			
5h	•	•								•						

Links to Other National Curriculum Subjects

Photograph		English	Science	History	Geography	RE
1a	Helping	•		•	•	•
1b	Welcoming a Visitor	•		•	•	•
2	Using Sign Language	•				
3a	Excluding	•				•
3b	Including	•				•
4	Sharing Special Occasions	•	•	•		•
5	Explaining Culture	•		•	•	•
6	Caring for the Environment	•	•		•	
7a	Discussing in Pairs	•				
7b	Working in Pairs	•				
8	Debating	•		•		
9	School Council Meeting	•		•		•
10a	Making School Rules	•		•		•
10b	Making Safety Rules	•		•	•	•
11	Voting	•		•		
12	Being a European Citizen	•		•	•	

Background Information for Teachers

Your Local Authority
(Photographs 1, 8, 11)

Everyone everywhere in the United Kingdom has a local authority. However, mainly for historical reasons, there are a number of different types. Depending on where you live, you may have a unitary authority, a metropolitan borough or a London borough. In other areas there are two tiers of local government, a county council and a district, borough or city council. In rural districts, there may also be parish or town councils or both.

Traditionally, local authorities raised funds locally through the rates; these funds were then spent on local services. This relationship has largely disappeared as funding now comes mainly from central government, despite the council tax. The spending plans of local authorities are largely controlled by central government.

Local authorities provide services such as education, housing, social services, planning, libraries, parks and playgrounds, refuse collection, environmental health, community centres and highway maintenance. The Local Agenda 21 Co-ordinator is also based with your local council. His or her remit, which comes from the Rio Earth Summit, is to help communities, including schools, plan for the future.

Elections to local authorities happen regularly but the intervals vary according to the type of authority. Elections generally occur every four years, but in some district councils a third of the members are elected every three years to give rolling changes. In the fourth year, the county councils are elected. Local councillors decide spending priorities within strict guidelines and take up matters with the council on behalf of local constituents. Councillors, especially those who are also school governors, are usually willing to help schools. The Mayor or Chairperson of the Council is the ceremonial leader for one or two years and he or she will usually visit a number of schools. Except where a council is hung, the leader is the head of the majority political party.

The councillors, including the Mayor or Chairperson, debate in the council chamber and in a number of smaller committees responsible for particular services. Councillors do not receive a salary but are paid an allowance. They are not to be confused with the council officers, who are employed to do the work of the council, led by a Chief Executive. Officers, too, have a remit to inform and assist residents, including school children. They are usually very willing to arrange for children to visit the council chamber and to tell them something of their work. It would be advisable to contact the Chief Executive's Office or the Public Relations Officer for advice on whom to contact. Planning officers are often able to help schools with information on local environmental issues.

Using Sign Language
(Photograph 2)

British sign language is a visual-gestural language which uses hand shapes, facial expressions, gestures and body language to convey meaning. It has its own distinctive grammatical structure. The resource sheets on sign language show (1) the finger spelling of the letters of the alphabet, which are used to spell out names, and (2) the sign language gestures and facial expressions that are used for simple greetings and phrases. Further information may be obtained from the Royal National Institute for the Deaf (RNID), the British Deaf Association (BDA) and the National Deaf Children's Society (NDCS). (See the 'Contact List' on pages 43–44.)

Braille is a method of reading by touch, which was devised by Louis Braille in 1829. It uses tactile dots to represent letters, numbers and punctuation marks. The Braille resource sheet shows how Braille letters are made from raised dots, like the six dots on a domino. Braille can be written using a special typewriter, or wordprocessor and Braille printer. You can obtain a Braille chart and further information on Braille and other communication methods used by blind and partially sighted people from the Royal National Institute for the Blind (RNIB). (See the 'Contact List' on page 44.)

Explaining Culture
(Photographs 4 and 5)

Citizenship education includes developing an understanding of other cultures, their similarities and differences. The Muslim faith and culture is used here as an example and reflects the diversity of cultures found in primary schools in Luton where this resource was developed. For some children the content of the photographs will be familiar; for others it will be new and different. The photographs will provide a starting point from which to explore our multicultural society. A calendar showing the dates of major religious festivals, with an information booklet briefly describing each one, can be obtained from The Shap Working Party on World Religions in Education. (See the 'Contact List' on page 44.)

There are 960 million Muslims in the world, of whom 1.5 million live in UK. The faith is based on the revelations of the prophet Mohammed (pbuh). ('Pbuh' is the written abbreviation of the words 'Peace be upon him', spoken after Mohammed's name by Muslims, as a mark of respect.) For Muslims, the words of the holy book, the Qur'an (or Koran), are the words of Allah (God) dictated directly to Mohammed. Mohammed first preached in Mecca (now in Saudi Arabia) and all Muslims, who are able and have the means, make a pilgrimage to Mecca once in their lifetime. Muslims pray five times each day, facing in the direction of Mecca (which is south-east from the UK). Some will carry a compass for this purpose, while others will use a prayer mat that incorporates a compass, like the one in the photograph. The Mosque is the public place of worship and there are over 650 Mosques in Britain.

During the sacred month of Ramadan, Muslims take part in ritual daylight fasting. At the festival of Eid ul-Fitr, which marks the end of this sacred month, Muslims send each other greetings cards, wear new clothes and share special food together.

Caring for the Environment
(Photograph 6)

Nature Garden
Schools are encouraged to develop all or part of their school grounds as a nature or wildlife garden. This is so that children may experience the natural world, observe wildlife in its natural habitat and learn to care for their environment. It is not recommended that the school keeps pets, but rather that insects, butterflies, birds and small mammals are encouraged to visit the school grounds. Children can take some responsibility for looking after the natural areas and learn to respect the plant and animal life therein. The nature garden should be seen as primarily a teaching resource, for other subjects as well as citizenship.

Many organisations can help schools plan, develop and manage their wildlife gardens, including The Wildlife Trusts and Learning through Landscapes. (See the 'Contact List' on pages 43–44.)

Environmental Policy
Schools are encouraged to work towards having an environmental policy, which can be built up gradually. The best school policies develop from lessons in science, maths and geography. For example, water conservation may be studied in geography, energy conservation in maths, recycling in science, a nature garden may be planned in geography and habitats studied in science. In addition, a school may set up an environmental action group to research the necessary changes and inform the rest of the school of plans. Later, the children could help to draft a code of practice for implementing the environmental policy.

A draft environmental policy to stimulate discussion might include some of the following aims:
- To care for the surroundings of the school
- To conserve water by remembering to turn off the taps
- To save energy by switching off lights and closing doors and windows

- To collect and recycle paper, glass and cans
- To put food waste in the compost bin
- To create habitats and learn to care for them
- To teach everyone the importance of caring for the environment

Organisations willing to help schools with this work include Eco-Schools and the Council for Environmental Education. (See the 'Contact List' on page 43.)

School Council Meeting
(Photograph 9)

As part of good practice in citizenship, it is recommended that schools set up class councils and a school council. It may be necessary for an adult to chair the council and to help with keeping minutes but the children should have as much ownership of their council as possible. All classes should be represented on the council, preferably by more than one child. They should be chosen by election for a fixed period and understand the need to represent the views of others and to report back.

The head teacher and teachers are ceding some of their authority to the council, so it needs to have a clear remit. It should be able to discuss and offer advice or raise matters of concern. Crucially, it should also be able to take decisions in certain well-defined areas. The power to spend a small amount of money might also encourage responsibility. A special project for each term or each year might give the council a necessary focus.

Schools Councils UK is a small charity that advises schools on setting up and running school councils. It provides resources including a video and training sessions for teachers. (See the 'Contact List' on page 44.)

Parliament
(Photographs 8, 10a,11)

Parliament is made up of the House of Commons and the House of Lords. There are currently 651 constituencies in the UK and each one elects an MP (Member of Parliament) as their representative in the House of Commons. A general election happens every five years or more frequently if the government chooses or is defeated in a motion of no confidence.

The majority party in the House of Commons is invited by the Queen to form the government. It is the government that takes decisions, which affect us all, but matters are debated and voted on in the Commons, so the size of the majority is important. Laws are made in parliament.

The Labour government elected in 1997 initiated significant constitutional change. There is now a Scottish Parliament in Edinburgh and a Welsh Assembly in Cardiff. The Scottish Parliament consists of 129 Members (MSPs), elected by the people of Scotland. The National Assembly for Wales consists of 60 Assembly Members (AMs), 40 of whom are elected by constituencies, with a further 20 being elected on a regional basis.

For many years there has been a debate about whether the House of Lords should be reformed. Voters in this country elect MPs, but until November 1999 members of the House of Lords were not elected and sat in Parliament because they had either received or inherited a title. The House of Lords Act 1999 removed the entitlement of most of the 750 hereditary peers to sit and vote in the House of Lords.

During a period of transition 92 hereditary peers, of which 75 were elected by their fellow hereditary peers, retain their seat in the Lords. This transitional chamber will exist until further reforms are implemented. The reforms recommended by the Royal Commission chaired by Lord Wakeham include the setting up of a new, mainly nominated, partly elected, chamber of around 550. The government has not committed itself to accepting any of the Commission's recommendations and at the present time there is no timetable for further reform.

The Parliamentary Education Unit will tell you which constituency your school is in and the name of the MP. (See the 'Contact List' on page 44.) He or she may well be interested in the citizenship work that your school is doing. You could invite the MP to a citizenship assembly. Friday is a good day as MPs are often in their constituency then.

European Union
(Photographs 8, 11, 12)

All UK citizens are also citizens of the European Union (EU). The EU has its origins in the European Economic Community (EEC) which was established in 1957 through the signing of the Treaty of Rome by six founder countries. Britain became a member in 1973, and there are now fifteen members of the European Union. The member states are Austria, Belgium, Denmark, Finland, France, Germany, Greece, Ireland, Italy, Luxembourg, Netherlands, Portugal, Spain, Sweden and UK. A further thirteen countries are hoping to join. There are over 370 million citizens in the European Union and eleven official languages.

The three main institutions of the EU are the European Commission, the Council of the European Union and the European Parliament. The European Commission consists of twenty members (commissioners) including two each from France, Germany, Italy, Spain and UK, and one from each of the other countries. It is independent of national governments, proposes laws and policies and oversees the implementation of policies across the EU.

The Council of the EU, usually referred to as the Council of Ministers, is made up of ministers from each member state. For example, the Council of Foreign Ministers is made up of the fifteen Foreign Ministers. The Council is responsible for legislation.

The European Parliament is directly elected by the citizens of all the member states. It consists of 626 MEPs (Members of the European Parliament), including 87 from the UK. The European Parliament, with the Council, adopts laws and gives approval to the appointment of the Commission.

Given the increasingly large part the EU plays in our lives, it is surprising that we have so little apparent interest in what goes on in Europe. The turnout at the elections to the European Parliament in June 1999 was low at 25 per cent of registered voters, lower than in any other member state. The need for citizenship education is obvious and should include the concept of European citizenship. If you want to know who the MEPs for your region are, contact the UK Office of the European Parliament. (See the 'Contact List' on page 43.)

Sources of Information for KS1 Citizenship

Information Required	Where to Obtain
Name of local authority/authorities	Local Education Authority or telephone directory
Type of council or councils	Local council
Number of councillors and wards	Local council
Services provided	Local council
Local elections, returning officer	Chief Executive, local council
Town Trail	Local museum or local library
Visits to local council chamber	Local council
Local environment	Planning department of local council Local Agenda 21 Co-ordinator at local council
Police	Education Liaison Officer, or Community Police Officer at your local police station
Fire Service	Local fire station
Parliament, Government	Parliamentary Education Unit (tel: 020 7219 4750)
European Parliament	UK Office (tel: 020 7227 4300)
United Nations	UNICEF UK (tel: 020 7405 5592)

Useful Organisations: Contact Details

The following organisations can help you find out more about specific areas of Infant Citizenship. Many of them provide resources, including some free materials, or catalogues, or background information or school liaison officers to visit your class, or INSET, or all of these. The best ways to find up-to-date information on what is available from each organisation are to visit their website or to write or telephone with your request.

ActionAid Education
Chataway House
Leach Road
Chard
Somerset
TA29 1FA
tel: 01460 62972
www.actionaid.org.uk

British Deaf Association (BDA)
BDA Head Office
1–3 Worship Street
London
EC2A 2AB
tel (voice): 020 7588 3520
minicom: 020 7588 3529
www.bda.org.uk

Christian Aid
PO Box 100
London
SE1 7RT
tel: 020 7620 4444
www.christian-aid.org.uk

Christian Education Movement
Royal Buildings
Victoria Street
Derby
DE1 1GW
tel: 01332 296 655

Citizen 21 Project
Charter 88
16–24 Underwood Street
London
N1 7JQ
tel: 020 7684 3888
www.citizen21.org.uk

Citizenship Foundation
Ferroners House
Shaftesbury Place
Aldersgate Street
London
EC2Y 8AA
tel: 020 7367 0500
www.citfou.org.uk

Commission for Racial Equality
Elliot House
10–12 Allington Street
London
SW1E 5EH
tel: 020 7828 7022
www.cre.gov.uk

Commonwealth Institute
Kensington High Street
London
W8 5EH
tel: 020 7603 4535
www.commonwealth.org.uk

Community Service Volunteers (CSV)
237 Pentonville Road
London
N1 9NJ
tel: 020 7278 6601
www.csv.org.uk

Consumers' Association
2 Marylebone Road
London
NW1 4DF
tel: 020 7770 7000
www.which.net

Council for Education in World Citizenship
15 St. Swithin's Lane
London
EC4N 8AL
tel: 020 7929 5090
www.cewc.org.uk

Council for Environmental Education
94 London Street
Reading
RG1 4SJ
tel: 0118 950 2550
www.cee.org.uk

DeafSign.Com
16 Highfield Crescent
Hartburn
Stockton on Tees
Cleveland
TS18 5HH
tel (voice/minicom): 01642 580505
www.deafsign.com

Eco-Schools
Tidy Britain Group
The Pier
Wigan
WN3 4EX
tel: 01942 824 620
www.tidybritain.org.uk

The Education Network
22 Upper Woburn Place
London
WC1H 0TB
tel: 020 7554 2810
www.ednet.org.uk

The European Commission
8 Storey's Gate
London
SW1P 3AR
tel: 020 7973 1992
www.cec.org.uk

The European Parliament
2 Queen Anne's Gate
London
SW1H 9AA
tel: 020 7227 4300
www.europarl.eu.int/uk

Friends of the Earth
26–28 Underwood Street
London
N1 7JQ
tel: 020 7490 1555
www.foe.co.uk

Geographical Association
160 Solly Street
Sheffield
S1 4BF
tel: 0114 296 0088
www.geography.org.uk

Institute for Citizenship
62 Marylebone High Street
London
W1M 5HZ
tel: 020 7935 4777
www.citizen.org.uk

The Institute for Global Ethics
17 Nottingham Street
London
W1M 3RD
tel: 020 7486 1954
www.globalethics.org

Learning through Landscapes
Third Floor, Southside Offices
The Law Courts
Winchester
Hampshire
SO23 9DL
tel: 01962 846 258
www.ltl.org.uk

Magistrates' Association
28 Fitzroy Square
London
W1P 6DD
tel: 020 7387 2353
www.magistrates-association.co.uk

The National Assembly for Wales
The Public Information and
Education Service
Cardiff Bay
Cardiff
CF99 1NA
tel: 029 20 898200
www.wales.gov.uk

National Consumer Council
20 Grosvenor Gardens
London
SW1W 0DH
tel: 020 7730 3469
www.ncc.org.uk

**National Deaf Children's Society
(NDCS)**
15 Dufferin Street
London
EC1V 8PD
tel: 020 7250 0123
www.ndcs.org.uk

**National Education Business
Partnership Network**
c/o Smith Kline Beecham
11 Stoke Poges Lane
Slough
SL1 3NW
tel: 01753 502 370

Operation Black Vote
16–24 Underwood Street
London
N1 7JQ
tel: 020 7684 3860
www.obv.org.uk

**Oxfam Development Education
and Resources Centre**
4th Floor
4 Bridge Place
London
SW1V 1XY
tel: 020 7931 7660
www.oxfam.org.uk/coolplanet

Parliamentary Education Unit
Room 604
Norman Shaw Building North
London
SW1A 2TT
tel: 020 7219 4750
www.explore.parliament.uk

**Royal National Institute for the
Blind (RNIB)**
224 Great Portland Street
London
W1N 6AA
tel: 020 7388 1266
www.rnib.org.uk

**Royal National Institute for the
Deaf (RNID)**
19–23 Featherstone Street
London
EC1Y 8SL
tel: 020 7296 8199
www.rnid.org.uk

**Royal Society for Prevention of
Cruelty to Animals (RSPCA)**
Causeway
Horsham
West Sussex
RH12 1HG
tel: 01403 264181
www.rspca.org.uk

**Royal Society for the Protection
of Birds (RSPB)**
The Lodge
Sandy
Bedfordshire
SG19 2DL
tel: 01767 680 551
www.rspb.org.uk

Save The Children Education
17 Grove Road
London
SE5 8DR
tel: 020 7703 5400
www.savethechildren.org.uk

Schools Council UK
57 Etchingham Park Road
London
N3 2EB
tel: 020 8349 2459

The Scottish Parliament
Edinburgh
EH99 1SP
tel: 0131 348 5000
www.scottish.parliament.uk

**The Shap Working Party on
World Religions in Education**
c/o The National Society's RE
Centre
36 Causton Street
London
SW1P 4AU
tel: 020 7932 1194
www.namss.org.uk/fests.htm

UNICEF UK
55 Lincoln Inn Fields
London
WC2A 3NB
tel: 020 7405 5592
www.unicef.org.uk

United Nations
Global Teaching and Learning
Project
c/o Cyberschoolbus
1 United Nations Plaza
Room DC1-552
New York NY10017
USA
www.un.org/Cyberschoolbus

The Wildlife Trusts
UK National Office
The Green, Witham Park
Waterside South
Lincoln
LN5 7JR
tel: 01522 544 400
www.wildlifetrust.org.uk

**World Wide Fund for Nature
(WWF)**
Panda House
Weyside Park
Godalming
Surrey
GU7 1XR
tel: 01483 426 444
www.wwf-uk.org

Websites

Global Cities
www.global-cities.org

National Grid for Learning
www.ngfl.gov.uk

SchoolNet
www.schoolnet.org.uk

YouthNet UK
www.thesite.org

**The Young People's Parliament
(YPP)**
www.ypp.org.uk

**World Wide List of Online
Newspapers**
www.onlinenewspapers.com

Extract from *The National Curriculum – Handbook for primary teachers in England*: 'Framework for personal, social and health education and citizenship at key stages 1 and 2'

The importance of personal, social and health education and citizenship

Personal, social and health education (PSHE) and citizenship help to give pupils the knowledge, skills and understanding they need to lead confident, healthy, independent lives and to become informed, active, responsible citizens. Pupils are encouraged to take part in a wide range of activities and experiences across and beyond the curriculum, contributing fully to the life of their school and communities. In doing so they learn to recognise their own worth, work well with others and become increasingly responsible for their own learning. They reflect on their experiences and understand how they are developing personally and socially, tackling many of the spiritual, moral, social and cultural issues that are part of growing up. They also find out about the main political and social institutions that affect their lives and about their responsibilities, rights and duties as individuals and members of communities. They learn to understand and respect our common humanity, diversity and differences so that they can go on to form the effective, fulfilling relationships that are an essential part of life and learning.

Key Stage 1

During key stage 1, pupils learn about themselves as developing individuals and as members of their communities, building on their own experiences and on the early learning goals for personal, social and emotional development. They learn the basic rules and skills for keeping themselves healthy and safe and for behaving well. They have opportunities to show they can take some responsibility for themselves and their environment. They begin to learn about their own and other people's feelings and become aware of the views, needs and rights of other children and older people. As members of a class and school community, they learn social skills such as how to share, take turns, play, help others, resolve simple arguments and resist bullying. They begin to take an active part in the life of their school and its neighbourhood.

The following are non-statutory guidelines.

Knowledge, skills and understanding

Developing confidence and responsibility and making the most of their abilities
1 Pupils should be taught:
   a to recognise what they like and dislike, what is fair and unfair, and what is right and wrong
   b to share their opinions on things that matter to them and explain their views
   c to recognise, name and deal with their feelings in a positive way
   d to think about themselves, learn from their experiences and recognise what they are good at
   e how to set simple goals.

Preparing to play an active role as citizens
2 Pupils should be taught:
   a to take part in discussions with one other person and the whole class

b to take part in a simple debate about topical issues
c to recognise choices they can make, and recognise the difference between right and wrong
d to agree and follow rules for their group and classroom, and understand how rules help them
e to realise that people and other living things have needs, and that they have responsibilities to meet them
f that they belong to various groups and communities, such as family and school
g what improves and harms their local, natural and built environments and about some of the ways people look after them
h to contribute to the life of the class and school
i to realise that money comes from different sources and can be used for different purposes.

Developing a healthy, safer lifestyle

3 Pupils should be taught:
a how to make simple choices that improve their health and well-being
b to maintain personal hygiene
c how some diseases spread and can be controlled
d about the process of growing from young to old and how people's needs change
e the names of the main parts of the body
f that all household products, including medicines, can be harmful if not used properly
g rules for, and ways of, keeping safe, including basic road safety, and about people who can help them to stay safe.

Developing good relationships and respecting the differences between people

4 Pupils should be taught:
a to recognise how their behaviour affects other people
b to listen to other people, and play and work co-operatively
c to identify and respect the differences and similarities between people
d that family and friends should care for each other
e that there are different types of teasing and bullying, that bullying is wrong, and how to get help to deal with bullying.

Breadth of Opportunities

5 During the key stage, pupils should be taught the **Knowledge, skills** and **understanding** through opportunities to:
a take and share responsibility (for example, for their own behaviour; by helping to make classroom rules and following them; by looking after pets well)
b feel positive about themselves (for example, by having their achievements recognised and by being given positive feedback about themselves)
c take part in discussions (for example, talking about topics of school, local, national, European, Commonwealth and global concern, such as 'where our food and raw materials for industry come from')
d make real choices (for example, between healthy options in school meals, what to watch on television, what games to play, how to spend and save money sensibly)
e meet and talk with people (for example, with outside visitors such as religious leaders, police officers, the school nurse)

f   develop relationships through work and play (for example, by sharing equipment with other pupils or their friends in a group task)

g   consider social and moral dilemmas that they come across in everyday life (for example, aggressive behaviour, questions of fairness, right and wrong, simple political issues, use of money, simple environmental issues)

h   ask for help (for example, from family and friends, midday supervisors, older pupils, the police).

**Extract from the Crick Report: *Education for Citizenship and the Teaching of Democracy in Schools*
Final report of the Advisory Group on Citizenship (22 September 1998), QCA**

Appendix 2

The learning outcomes for Key Stage 1

6 .11.1 Skills and Aptitudes

By the end of Key Stage 1, pupils should be able to:

- express and justify orally a personal opinion relevant to an issue;

- contribute to paired and class discussion on matters of personal and general significance, learning what it means to take turns, respond to the views of others and use acceptable forms of disagreement or challenge;

- work with others and gather their opinions in an attempt to meet a challenge of shared significance;

- use imagination when considering the experience of others;

- reflect on issues of social and moral concern, presented in different ways such as through story, drama, pictures, poetry, and 'real life' incidents;

- take part in a simple debate and vote on an issue.

6.11.2 Knowledge and Understanding

By the end of Key Stage 1, pupils should:

- recognise how the concept of fairness can be applied in a reasoned and reflective way to aspects of their personal and social life;

- understand the different kinds of responsibility that they take on, in helping others, respecting differences or looking after shared property;

- know about the nature and basis of the rules in the classroom, at school and at home; also, whenever possible, know how to frame rules themselves; understand that different rules can apply in different contexts and can serve different purposes, including safety, safeguarding of property and the prevention of unacceptable behaviour;

- know about the different kinds of relationships which exist between pupils and between adults and pupils; also have some notion that the power in such relationships can be exercised responsibly and fairly or irresponsibly and unfairly;

- understand the language used to describe feelings associated with aspects of relationships with others, including words such as *happy*, *sad*, *disappointed*, *angry*, *upset*, *shy*, *embarrassed*, *peaceful*, *worried*, *proud* and *glad*;

- understand different kinds of behaviour using moral categories such as *kind* or *unkind*, *good* or *bad*, *right* or *wrong*; know about the consequences of anti-social or egocentric behaviour and attitudes, for individuals and communities; also understand that many problems can be tackled as a community;

- know where they live, in relation to their local and national community, understand that there are different types and groups of people living in their local community such as other children, teenagers, families and old people;

- know about differences and similarities between people in terms of their needs, rights, responsibilities, wants, likes, values and beliefs; also understand that many of these differences are linked with cultural and religious diversity;

- know and understand, through shared activities and the process of exploratory talk, the meaning of key terms such as *respect* or *disrespect*, *question*, *comment*, *discuss*, *agree* or *disagree*, *similar* or *different*, *point of view*, *opinion*, *compare* and *contrast*.